Inside/Out:

Continuing to Cage Your Rage

Murray Cullen, Ph.D. and
Michael Bradley, Ph.D.

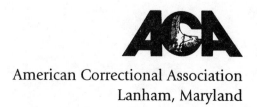

American Correctional Association
Lanham, Maryland

American Correctional Association Staff

Hon. Betty Adams Green, President
James A. Gondles, Jr., CAE, Executive Director
Gabriella M. Daley, Director, Communications and Publications
Harry Wilhelm, Marketing Manager
Alice Fins, Publications Managing Editor
Michael Kelly, Associate Editor
Anne Hasselbrack, Editorial Assistant
Dana M. Murray, Graphics and Production Manager
Book production by Capitol Communication Systems, Inc.
Cover by Mike Selby

Printed in the United States of America by Graphic Communications Inc., Upper Marlboro, MD.

For information on publications and videos available from ACA, contact our world-wide web home page at: http://www.corrections.com/aca

ISBN-1-56991-136-3

This publication may be ordered from:
American Correctional Association
4380 Forbes Boulevard
Lanham, Maryland 20706-4322
1-800-222-5646

Contents

Foreword

A Few Words About the Process: Road Map to a Better Life

This is your book. Write directly in this book. Be honest in what you write. Some people have completed *Cage Your Rage*. Some of you may not have. This is okay.

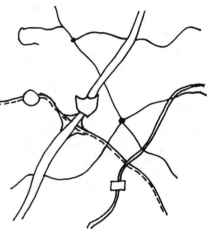

The first *Cage Your Rage* workbook was your diary, a work-in-progress, about you! This was your special book. You were not required to show others the written assignments and personal notes on yourself, unless you were willing to do so. The goal of the work was to start you making changes so that you could have a better life.

It is important that, in this current book, you again have the choice of keeping your material confidential. At the very least, this can be considered a self-help book for you. If you are reading this as part of an individual counseling plan or as part of an anger management program, consider sharing your insights and work with others. The people who are working with you are doing so for a common cause—to help you manage your anger and be more in control of your life! These traits controlling your anger and your life are important while you are incarcerated, and they are vital when you are out.

If you are in a group program, be sure that anything that you learn about the other participants remains confidential. You cannot tell others outside the group what you have learned about others. You must respect the privacy of other participants. This is especially important if you are expecting them to respect your confidences. If you are working individually with counselors, trust and confide in them. The counselors are trying to help you be a better person and have a better life than you have had in the past.

For this program to help you, you need to complete the exercises! The questions in this manual were chosen for a reason. They all need to be completed. You have to complete the exercises in a written form for you to get the maximum benefit of control over your anger. Use this workbook. Study it. Treasure it. Confide in it. When you have completed reading and doing all the exercises, this book will serve as a personal guide or road map to allow you to travel to a better life. Have a good journey!

Chapter 1

A Short Trip Down Memory Lane

Some of you may have worked through the exercises in *Cage Your Rage*. However, even if you have not, we will provide a summary of the contents to help you. If you have gone through the *Cage Your Rage* workbook, then this should be a handy review for you. If, however, you would like to get a copy of this book and do the exercises in it, copies of *Cage Your Rage* may be purchased from the American Correctional Association at the address on the back of the title page.

In *Cage Your Rage*, we talked about what happens when you get angry. We described the ABCs of anger arousal. The "A" stands for the event that arouses your anger. "B" stands for the belief or self-talk (what you say to yourself) about the situation, and "C" stands for the consequences of your self-talk, your actions. For example, an elderly woman "inches" herself ahead of you in a grocery store checkout line. Her action is the activating event "A." Saying to yourself "that old lady is showing me disrespect and playing me for a fool" represents the "B"; tapping her on the shoulder and saying "Hey you, get to the back of the line" represents the "C" of your beliefs.

In the spaces below, write out two other sets of ABCs for the grocery line situation.

A _____

B _____

C _____

A _____

B _____

C _____

We talked about "thinking" controls, or ways to prevent negative thought patterns such as the following:

Common Thinking Mistakes

1. **All or Nothing Thinking.** You see things as all right or all wrong, black or white. If your case management officer said she would see you on Thursday and did not, then you think she never wants to see you.

2. **Overgeneralizing.** You view one bad situation as a never-ending pattern of bad situations. If you were picked on while going to supper, you want to avoid going to supper because you think you always will get picked on.

3. **Using a Mental Filter.** You pick out one bad thing and dwell on it to the point that everything seems bad. The only things that filter in are bad things.

4. **Not Counting on the Good Things.** When something good happens to you, you say it was just luck. When something bad happens to you, you consider it normal. You might say, "Yeah, I got a letter from my mother this week, but she has really forgotten all about me."

5. **Jumping to Conclusions.** This happens when you decide that something is bad even though you do not know for sure.

   a. **Mind Reading.** You think that someone dislikes you, and you do not bother to check it out. For example, you are walking across the recreation yard and notice that a staff member seems to be looking at you. Because he is staring, you think he does not like you. In fact, he is staring into space and thinking about something else and not paying any attention to you.

   b. **The Fortune Teller Mistake.** You believe that something will turn out badly and it does. You believe you are going to be denied parole. This ends up coming true because you go into the parole meeting feeling lousy. You think the board has judged you already. Because of your bad attitude, you make a bad impression, and the board says you are not ready for release. You have cut your own throat.

6. **Magnifying or Minimizing.** This is called the binocular trick. When something good happens, you think it does not count. You tend to minimize it, like looking through binoculars backwards. Everything

good looks smaller. Bad events become magnified, like looking through the binoculars the right way. A small problem seems bigger, and you spend more time dwelling on it.

7. **Reasoning How You Feel.** An example would be, "Because I feel bad, there must be bad things happening to me. There must be a reason for me to feel bad. If not, I might as well make one up." This could lead you to dwell on bad things.

8. **Using "Should" Statements.** You say, "I should" or "I shouldn't", "I must" or "I ought" in your talk. "I should have taken that course or I should have done my job better. I must write home today." Such talk makes you feel guilty. There was probably a good reason why you did not do it. More problems occur when you direct "shoulds, musts, and oughts" toward others. You feel frustrated, resentful, and angry because people do not behave like you want. Bad self-talk might be, "He should have passed me the salt. He never thinks about me. He doesn't like me. He's no hotshot. I don't like him either."

9. **Labeling and Mislabeling.** When you do something wrong, you might say , "I never get anything right, I'm always wrong, I'm a loser." Mislabeling occurs when you describe an event, either to yourself, or to others in a way that is full of feeling that convinces others or yourself how important that event was, and it usually makes the situation worse.

10. **Taking it Personally.** You take the blame for some bad event even though it was not your fault. "It's my fault she's sick. I should not have asked her to come over." "It's my fault there was a fight in the cellblock last night. I'm a jinx and I bring trouble wherever I go." "It's my fault; I had a brew last night and today the prison is on lockdown."

Think of times over the last week that you might have employed one or more of these thinking mistakes. Name the thinking error, describe what you thought, and tell why it was not the best approach.

_____

_____

_____

_____

_____

_____

_____

_____

_____

_____

_____

Thought Stopping

Your body gives you certain body cues that indicate you are becoming angry. You can recognize these feelings that indicate you are becoming angry. Use these cues to slow down and consider what is happening and to consider what you are saying to yourself before you respond to the situation.

Think of a recent situation where thought stopping or slowing down your reactions was or would have been valuable to you.

_____

_____

_____

Staging

You deal with an anger-provoking situation one step at a time. The steps include (1) preparing for the situation, (2) assessing the impact of the situation, (3) coping with your feelings, and (4) reflecting on the experience afterwards.

Think of a recent situation when you became angry. Consider the situation and explain how using these staging steps would have helped you.

_____

_____

_____

_____

We talked about "feeling" controls. One control for your body includes training in relaxation. Another control for your mind involves keeping in good humor. We also discussed the importance of communicating your feelings honestly, and attempting to calm down the other person. We even asked you to make a first attempt at identifying some thoughts, feelings, and behaviors that would let you know when you were becoming angry. What thoughts and body sensations occur when you are getting angry? Write them in the spaces below.

Thoughts

_____

_____

_____

_____

_____

Body Sensations

_____

_____

_____

_____

_____

Cage Your Rage did not talk much about what to "do" or "how to behave" when you are becoming angry. It did talk about relaxation methods to help you try and stay calm. Briefly, they included:

(1) taking deep breaths

(2) pausing and reflecting before answering important questions— this may involve counting slowly to ten

(3) keeping yourself calm with self-talk

(4) listening to relaxation tapes

6

(5) learning the muscle "tense and release" cycle

(6) using imagery for relaxation; imagine yourself taking a stroll through a garden or walking along a beach

Cage Your Rage discussed anger logs. These anger logs were your quick written reports that accurately documented the particulars of an anger situation and explained how you dealt with it. These anger logs can help you to reflect on the situation (analyze it afterwards) and learn how to handle a similar situation more appropriately for the next time.

But . . . to really apply yourself to the tasks ahead, you must prepare yourself now to make a commitment to change. Up until this point, you might have been living in a "rat race." You followed the prison routine—were awakened in the morning, had your breakfast, went to your job, came back to your living quarters, sat and watched TV at night, and so forth until you went to bed and woke up the next morning to do the same dull routine over and over, and over again. Life was possibly not very satisfying. If something went wrong, you did not have either the energy or motivation to fix it. On the outside, a similar scenario could have played itself out. Maybe, you were too busy trying to keep up with everyone else: trying to keep your bills paid, trying to keep everyone else happy, or attempting to make it through to the next paycheck.

You might have figured that your life was all right, nothing really glamorous or wonderful, but still, not bad. You had some money for drinking or for fun or for whatever hobby that you liked to do. Still, you might have been in a bit of a "rut," so into "doing" the same routine that it would be difficult and take a great deal of energy on your part to change anything in your life. After all, why should you change? You worked hard, you deserved to have a rest and have some fun at the end of the week, and not everything in life was going your way anyway. So, why would you have to make any changes or owe anybody anything? No, you just decided to live your life from day to day.

Because of the way that you were living before, you made some bad choices. Perhaps you also made some bad choices while incarcerated. Those choices led to violence or some other legal problem. That is reason enough to change. You probably did not like the person you had become at the time you were aggressive. And probably you hurt not only your victim, but others in your life (wife, husband, children, parents, brothers, sisters, and others).

You also may have hurt yourself by going through the court process, by being put in jail, by being humiliated, and by losing your job and career, and maybe more. That was just for starters. You may have been locked up and had your freedom taken away! Now, people may have a great deal of difficulty trusting you. Your family may not be supportive of you anymore.

It may seem to you that the people who provide individual counseling or who lead you through anger programs want you to find out what has gone wrong in your life. They seem to dwell on details of your aggression, and they seem to "bully" you or make you feel even worse about what you did. Despite what you may believe, the reason you are asked to go through the exercises is not to feel worse. The reason is that you have to find out what went wrong in your life. What allowed you to cross over the legal and moral boundaries to allow yourself to be aggressive to others?

Even though you knew your violent behavior was wrong, somehow you convinced yourself that it was all right for you to do what you did. What terrible and ugly thoughts, feelings, and behaviors led up to your violent acts? What thoughts, feelings, and behaviors allowed you to justify the things you did as not so bad?

As you find out what went wrong in your life, you also will be finding out how you stumbled in the past and how you made bad mistakes. Through this knowledge, you will be able to avoid bad choices in the future. Thus, there will not be any other victims (including yourself). All of this should be reason enough for you to change.

Unlike rats always racing to some imaginary finish line, you will learn to slow down, think, and start concentrating on small tasks. These small tasks include the specific personal growth assignments, which are the written exercises in this book. Slowing down is very important since taking your time is the first key to beating the rat race.

Consider each item in the following list. Provide an example in which you ignored that point, and explain how you could improve on it in the future. If you need additional space you can staple additional blank pages to the pages in the book.

1. **Spending the Right Amount of Time**—Slow down and think things out. Do not hurry yourself, and do not let other people hurry you!

_____

_____

_____

_____

2. **Being Honest**—Be honest with yourself and with others. Sometimes it is difficult to be truthful, but it is extremely important for you to be honest. Dishonesty contributed to your acting out with violent behavior. So, be honest! It is a hard habit to start, but once you are honest, behaving honestly will come more easily.

_____

_____

_____

_____

3. **Making an Effort**—For any change to occur, you have to put effort into it. You have to invest not only time but energy. Look, for example, at people who work on cars for a hobby. They put a lot of time, money, and effort into what they do (rebuilding that old Chevy with the fins, and so forth). The same thing goes for people who are weekend carpenters. They have much expensive equipment and spend a great deal of time in their basement or workshop making toys, bookshelves, and other things. All of this takes a great deal of effort. When you invest effort into doing something, it becomes worthwhile for you to do it, and over time, the amount of energy it takes to do something decreases. In other words, with effort, the amount of time you need to spend on something lessens.

_____

_____

_____

_____

4. **Rationalizing Your Actions**—Rationalizations are the justifications or explanations you give to yourself. In your case, there is a chance that many of your justifications for violent behavior were really defense mechanisms. You might have blamed others, blamed alcohol or drugs, or provided excuses for why what you did was not so bad. Whenever you provide or hear a rationalization or "explanation," always ask yourself if that is a good explanation or simply something to cover up what you or someone else should not have done.

_____

_____

_____

_____

5. **Being Aware**—It is VERY important to be alert to everything that is going on with you. Be aware of what your thoughts, feelings, and behaviors are. Think of somebody spilling coffee on you by accident while you were sitting at a food court in a local mall. If you knew the person and liked him, the chances are that you would think it was an accident and you would feel less angry than if it were somebody whom you did not know or like. In that case, you might think that the person spilled a drink on you on purpose and you would feel extremely angry. Another example may be a sudden collision between you and some person while walking down a crowded street. Your reaction depends on your mood and circumstances. Be aware of your feelings and thoughts. They are what steer your behavior, for good or bad!

Provide two examples where you reacted the way that you did because you were in:

(a)   an extremely good mood

_____

_____

(b)   an extremely bad mood

_____

_____

In the last case, how might you have reacted if you had been in a good mood?

_____

_____

_____

_____

_____

_____

6. **Trusting**—You have to start relying on people. Trust is not something that you can develop overnight. It takes a long while for you to develop trust in someone—including yourself. However, you are in a bad situation now and unfortunately, at the time of your violence, you could not even trust yourself. If you could have trusted yourself, you might not have been aggressive, abusive, or violent, and faced all of these consequences. You have to start trusting somebody now. You might as well give your anger-management group a chance. The purpose of the group is to help you understand why you committed your assaults. What went wrong in your life? It seems in your best interest to start working with the group and to start having confidence in the group, even if it is only a bit at a time.

_____

_____

_____

_____

7. **Risk taking**—Many of us have a "comfort zone." While we are there, everything goes well and we feel very comfortable. When we are required to go out of our comfort zone, for example, to give a speech to a roomful of people, we no longer are comfortable. We would much rather stay in our little zone where everything is safe and be where we do not have to take any risks. Whenever we risk something, there is the chance that we will lose. There is a strong feeling within each of us not to take risks.

That is too bad. However, we have been taking risks all our lives. As we were growing up, we started taking risks, like being without our moms and dads for short periods of time. We went to school and learned to trust other people, such as a teacher or coach. We developed friendships and started relying on other people our age. Sometimes these risks helped us. Sometimes they did not.

However, taking risks, despite the fact that you may not like to do so, is a necessary part of living in today's society. You must learn to start taking risks. The particular risks that will help you involve being truthful and honest, being able to look at yourself and look at the lies that you told yourself, and admitting those lies to the group. Only when you get the lies out into the open and discuss them with people who are supportive of you, can you deal with the issues that make your life difficult. You are going to have to start taking risks and give out information that you have kept secret.

For example, perhaps you were sexually abused. Perhaps you were betrayed in some important way by someone you thought was on your side. You may never have told anyone because of the potential embarrassment this could lead to and also because you feel so uncomfortable and humiliated just being reminded of it, let alone describing your experience in detail to someone else.

Keeping these kinds of secrets exacts a toll on you. It makes you bitter and twisted. Over time, these secrets help you build up walls of defense between yourself and others. The result is that you no longer want to trust, try, or take risks. That attitude stops your growth as an individual. It stops your learning. More importantly, it blocks positive experiences and the fun that you should have in your life.

_____

_____

_____

_____

8. **Accepting the negative**—If you are going to do well in this treatment program, you must be very honest and tell things that are not so positive about yourself. You may receive criticism about your past behavior or your past thoughts or feelings. REMEMBER, the group will be criticizing those things and not you as a person! As an individual, you are worthwhile and have many good points. It is what you did in the past (violence and abuse) that neither the group nor society can approve. You hurt somebody very deeply, and that cannot be changed. You must accept the fact that you have done some terrible wrongs when you were angry. You may not like everything that is said about you during the course of the program. When you give the group information that they find negative, they will point it out to you. This is part of the treatment process. For you, or for anybody, to grow, you have to accept some feedback. Not all of the feedback may be good. Yet, you must accept it, not fight it. Accepting the feedback is a way of improving your outlook on life.

_____

_____

_____

_____

12

9. **Checking yourself** (Staying on top)—Keep all of the things previously discussed in this book in mind. Keep checking yourself out and fight your old ways of thinking. They are old defense mechanisms and false justifications. Be more aware of bad or inappropriate thoughts or feelings that you have. Keep yourself "honest." Although this is a difficult process to do at first, it gets much easier after awhile. By checking yourself, you will become better able to detect your inappropriate thoughts or feelings. You will be able to think of something to do right away to deal with your anger. By checking yourself, you can stay on top of the situation and make sure nothing bad comes out as a result.

_____

_____

_____

_____

10. **Being Emotionally Aware**—Become aware of your emotions. This is not quite as easy as you might think. People have primary and secondary emotions. Often people react to their secondary emotions without even realizing that they have primary emotions. Primary emotions are the first reactions you have to an exciting event, whether it is upsetting or pleasant. These primary emotions then change into secondary emotions. This change can be so automatic that people hardly realize what has happened to them.

For example, if you are at a dance with a girlfriend, and she is on the dance floor with another fellow, you become angry with her. That anger is a secondary emotion. At first, you actually felt one, some, or all of the following: insecurity, embarrassment, confusion, and "hurt" (probably your pride). Because you did not know how to handle these emotions, you became angry. Unfortunately, you do know what to do when you are angry. You can exhibit all kinds of thoughts and behaviors. You can be verbally insulting to her and physically assaultive towards the other man. We say "unfortunately you know what to do when you are angry" because you used violence and aggression. This got you in trouble.

Of course, you want to stop using anger and violence in the ways you have in the past that got you into trouble. The sooner you can become aware of your primary feelings, and stay with those initial feelings, the sooner you can avoid many of the old problems. Many situations or problems in your life can be dealt with earlier on, before there are any problems. Your new emotional awareness can give you a great advantage over the way you used to be.

Yet, it is going to take some effort to deal directly with your primary emotions. Primary emotions are those you do not like to admit to having. They did not suit your image as a competent, tough, and capable person. You often have thought of them as the emotions of vulnerability. Look at the boxes below and especially at the one marked Primary Emotions. These emotions do not have the kind of short-term reactions that you associate with the "cool" movie and TV "tough guys." For example, what do you do when you are embarrassed? Most people blush and look at their shoes. Are you embarrassed about being embarrassed?

Think about it. So what if you are embarrassed! Do not turn your embarrassment into a big troublesome drama, especially one that ends with your arrest.

Getting rearrested for your behavior is foolish. It leaves you ten times more vulnerable and less competent than when you can understand and express your true emotions In this book, you are going to find out what to do so you can avoid discomfort without converting everything to angry, bitter, and ultimately self-defeating emotions.

Look at the secondary emotions list. What a pile of trouble! As a former "tough guy," you used secondary emotions to present an image to

Primary Emotions	**Secondary Emotions**
confusion	anger
powerlessness	upset
shock	depression
helplessness	sadness
embarrassment	bitterness
hurt	vengefulness

others. You wanted to impress others to protect your ego and image. You found this image suited you and you lost sight of your own vulnerability while you got deeper into trouble. Now, you are able to drop the "fantasy character you have created" and "get real" by finding out and acting on your true feelings, your primary emotions. And, what is even better, you no longer will be afraid to show your true emotions. (More practice on distinguishing primary and secondary emotions is in Chapter 3.)

_____

_____

There is a lot to think about in these ten points and especially point number ten—being emotionally aware. Until now, you have not taken the time to think through who you actually are nor how to plan a good life for yourself and those you love. You, like so many other people in today's society, were living and running in "the rat race." You ran just to keep up. You did not know where the finish line was. You did not feel really happy, but you were not willing to change anything.

The ten points just discussed show you a way to get out of "the rat race" or, if you choose, the ten points will instruct you on how to win "the rat race" and have a successful life. To make it a bit easier for you to remember, the first letter from each of the ten points listed below spells out "The Rat Race."

Here is a review of the main points.

Time _____

_____

_____

Honesty _____

_____

_____

Effort _____

_____

_____

Rationalizations _____

_____

_____

Awareness _____

_____

_____

Trusting _____

_____

_____

Risk taking _____

_____

_____

Accepting of the negative _____

_____

_____

Checking yourself _____

_____

_____

Emotional Awareness

_____

_____

Now, go back and next to each of these words, write in your own words the main idea behind the concept. Then, go back and provide an example of how you could implement or put each of these items into practice.

Keeping all this information in mind, get ready to get down to some hard work. Provide answers to the following questions:

1. Why do I want to read this book?

_____

_____

2. What do I expect to gain from reading and completing the exercises in this book?

_____

_____

Now, if you are a guy and you are reading this, you may be thinking, "Why are they always singling us out? Women are just as aggressive! They have thrown punches at us; thrown dishes, beer bottles, pointed knives; and, there is nothing more vicious than a cat fight!" It is true that some women do act in an aggressive and vicious manner. However, most of what you read in the paper and what you see out in the streets is men being violent toward other men, women, children, and even animals. The issue here is not to point a finger of blame. Aggressive acts, done by men or women, are wrong, especially if they are done toward a friend or loved one!

The important issue and point of anger management is for you to take responsibility for your feelings. You can learn to deal with your feelings appropriately before they turn to anger and push you into aggressive behaviors.

Chapter 2

Dream Time Is Over—
The Street Beckons

You are or soon will be out of prison or out of a treatment program! What is going to happen to you? You no longer will be controlled by the prison system, the correctional officers, or the other inmates.

You can walk in the sunshine, climb that mountain, mingle with people on the streets, watch the wind play with the hair of that eye-catching person, shout into the wide-open spaces— all because you are free.

This is great! All the little dreams you had in prison, all the little joys that you once had and did not really notice . . . they are all yours again! The outside world is open to you.

Why? Because, you are free.

Now, dream time is over. This is or soon will be reality.

In this new reality, you have two major goals. One is to live your life in a way that brings satisfaction to you and those who are close to you. The other goal is to avoid going back to prison or jail.

List some of the things you want to do now that you are "free."

_____

_____

_____

_____

_____

_____

Who would you like to see and spend some time with now that you are "free"? Why?

_____

_____

_____

_____

You are free, but you are not totally free!

No one is ever totally free. You are just free of some things. You, for instance, are now free of prison, but that is it. Like everyone, you have restrictions and, in fact, due to parole conditions, you have more restrictions than most people. That may sound a little disappointing, but you can deal with it. You learned from prison, and now you know that some restrictions are good for you. They will make you think twice about doing things that could get you into trouble. You can get advice, information, and guidance about how you are adapting to life from your probation or parole services.

Think of parole as the solid double line on the highway. It always keeps you on your side of the road. Staying on your side of the line is a small price to pay to avoid wrecking yourself and others just to travel in the wrong lane.

List some activities that you like, which may get you into trouble.

_____

_____

_____

_____

_____

You are not free of yourself. You were free before prison, but your weaknesses or lack of judgment put you in prison. Are you going to follow the same path again? You worked on the trouble-making part of yourself in prison. You could control it there. It was easier to control yourself in prison, because everyone was watching you. In fact, the correctional officers got paid to watch your behavior, and the therapists got paid to watch your mind. You were a little job creation project. Now, it is up to you to watch you. And just like everyone else on the outside, you do not get paid for watching yourself.

You are capable of watching over yourself. In prison you had the practice run. You practiced how to control yourself, how to obey the rules, and even how to figure out what the rules were when they were not clearly written. You had taken anger management or you can take it. The difference between being in prison and being out is that outside, if you are not watching yourself, you might get away with something because no one is in your face watching you.

What you have learned, however, is that anything you get away with is the start of a trap that moves you down the wrong path or to continue the car analogy, into the wrong lane. If that happens, you are smart enough to know now that you had better turn around and get in the right lane. You are especially cautious now, because the temptations on the outside can be very strong. But you have resisted some pretty strong temptations in prison to get out. You can do the same thing once you get your head around the idea that resisting temptation will keep you out.

You are not free to go everywhere. It may be legal but some of your relatives, friends, and acquaintances will not make you welcome. They do not trust you. They are ashamed of you. They do not like your reputation. This is a huge disappointment. Maybe you can win back some of them, but others are lost to you for a long time. Although you probably could use their influence, you blew your relationship with them because of your past. Now, you will have to get by without them. Even people who talk to you will not always understand what you went through. They have not been to prison, so they do not understand and maybe do not want to understand. Your frustration is that some of the help you need is not going to be easily available. You will have to rely mostly on yourself and hope, somewhere along the line, people will give you a break

List some of the people you would like to see but who will not want to see you. List a reason why each one will not want to see you. Do you owe any of them an apology?

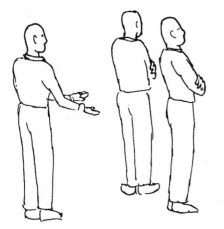

_____

_____

_____

_____

_____

_____

_____

Your dreams and expectations of how it is going to go on the outside are one of the biggest problems. Your dreams are fantasies, and in fantasies, we only dream the good parts. Life, in general, is hard. You were saying your dream is to walk in the sunshine when you were locked in prison. Now that you have done it, you have gotten a sunburn and sore feet! They were not part of the dream, but they are part of reality. You are rebuilding a life—your life. Good things are going to happen, but they may not be as good as the fantasy.

All real things have a down side. All real things bring duties and responsibilities. Your happiness, just like anyone else's, comes from the decision that seeking such happiness is worth the effort. Your job will give you money at the end of the week, but it requires time and effort. If you marry that special someone, she will want you to give up those other women, pay the bills, and treat her right. Your idea of happiness has to switch from what makes you happy to what makes both of you happy.

You may be more alone than you ever have been. It may be harder to make friends than before you were in prison. People may seem to react differently to you. You have to be prepared for that. It is not that they have changed. You have changed. You do not want to go back to your old ways of behaving, but it can be a shock to adjust. People are not going to treat you as well as you want them to, and they might treat you worse than you expected.

What you expect depends on what kind of con you were in the past. If you were a bully, people used to suck up to you. You used to intimidate them. They may have acted friendly even if they thought you were a turkey, because they were scared. Now that you are not using intimidation, they are not afraid to show their true feelings. Their lack of fear cuts two ways. Some people will not like you, but those who do will like you for yourself. They will be better and more reliable friends.

If you used to steal, people may have thought you were cool because you had stuff or could get them stuff. Now, you do not have things, so you are going only on your personality. They might think you have an untrustworthy, lousy personality because you are a thief (and ultimately a stupid one who got caught). Well, you are dropping the stupid and untrustworthy parts because you are not stealing anymore. You probably are going to drop the friends who benefitted from your theft because they also are untrustworthy. Your new friends or some old ones, who dropped you when you were stealing, will treat you better.

If it was drug dealing, the money, the highs, and the good times are not the same when you are older. Some of your former fun friends have matured out of it, or have burned out, or are still in it but do not look or feel so good. The ones who got out of it want nothing to do with you. They do not want temptations or reminders of that lifestyle. Those who are burned out, or are not doing so well, want to hang with you, but you know that they are desperate and are going to cause you trouble.

You are a different person now. The other ways of getting along were phony and got you some phony friends. Phony friends are people who will not stick by you. Now is your chance to find your true friends. People do not exist to live up to your expectations. They will not always act as you want them to act. You have to accept these limitations. You will find friends with whom you can get along. Friends will help you out from time to time, but not always. With your new friends, you have not bullied them or bought their loyalty. They just happen to like you, and you get along.

Remember how it was in prison? Everyone needed a buddy. If you were strong, people sought you for protection. You needed them for information, backup, and support. If you were weak, you needed protection. The big thing was that very few people, if any, could go it alone. That was so clear, and because of the danger, you traded what you could to get along with your group. In prison, maybe it was too much to trade, but you needed to and did it. In prison, you needed absolute loyalty and reliability 100 percent of the time. This has given you a distorted view of why you need a friend.

On the street, you can move away from big trouble. You still need friends and buddies but the danger is not there if you have gotten a good handle on your life. You do not have to give so much, and you cannot demand so much as in prison. Out on the street, you need a friend to tell a few jokes to, to give you a little companionship, to give you some advice, to help you find a job, to introduce you to new potential friends—maybe even to be that special someone.

What do you expect from a friend?

_____

_____

_____

_____

What should a friend expect from you?

_____

_____

_____

_____

_____

Write down the names of people you should avoid. Next to their names tell why you should avoid them. Will you get into trouble if you are around them?

_____

_____

_____

_____

_____

_____

_____

_____

_____

What is going to frustrate you if it does not go as you expect?

_____

_____

_____

_____

_____

Being alone on the "outside" is possible. It might even be a good thing from time to time. It gives you a chance to adjust without pressure. Your friends and relatives, even if they were trying, could not keep you out of trouble before. Some of your past friends actually may help pull you into trouble. Their habits and their lifestyle put trouble and temptation in your way. Maybe some are staying away from you because they know that the two of you together lose control. You have to respect that.

From now on, you should make new friends. You may not be as close, but these new friends will help you feel a little less lonely and maybe help show you how to live without getting in trouble with the law. There is support for cons. There will be individuals in the halfway house who honestly are trying to go straight. You might luck out and find a counselor you deeply respect. Church groups can give you companionship. Maybe, if you are lucky, when some time has gone by and you are doing fine, some of those friends who shunned you might give you another chance.

List some of the people or organizations that might give you support.

_____

_____

_____

_____

_____

_____

Self-love

"Nobody loves me like you love yourself." This is true for every human being whether saint or sinner. There also are problems with this self-love. We convince ourselves that we are deserving of good things by remembering the good deeds that we have done. We forget many of our bad characteristics. If we do remember a bad characteristic, we do two things. (1) We compare ourselves to people who are worse than we are in some ways. "Yeah, well at least I am not a goofball like Joe." (2) We think that the majority of people in our situation would act like we do. The thief says: "Everybody is on the take," without thinking that some people are very honest.

We like to say that others caused our misfortune. "I had a bad teacher and that is why I did not learn." "She made me do it," "How come I was the only one caught?" Yet, the reality is you know what you have to learn so it is your responsibility. You know the rules. Why should you break them? If you break them, why should you not get caught?

List some of the times you blamed others for your weaknesses or mistakes.

_____

_____

_____

_____

_____

List some of the times that you built yourself up by comparing yourself to people worse than you.

_____

_____

_____

_____

_____

Stop whining! Who said life is fair? It is not. You could be walking down the street as innocent as possible and "whap," you get run over by a car. Killed. You are dead and you did not do anything! Maybe worse, you get injured and are in pain for the rest of your life! So, bad things happen. You lose. Are you going to whine about your fate for the rest of your life or are you going to pick yourself up and go on? You could have been born 150 years ago and been tortured and hung for your crime. Or maybe you could have been born in a country where they let you go free for stealing but only after cutting off your fingers and branding your forehead.

Believe it or not, in the grand scheme of things, you are lucky! You know plenty of whiners. Sometimes it is a relief to whine and get some things off your chest. But you also know that whining gets you nowhere. People may give you a little sympathy, but you never really will get satisfaction from that. They only will give you as much sympathy as they think you deserve, and that is never as much as you think you should have.

Which types of people are you around when you get into trouble? What specific individuals were you around when you got into trouble?

_____

_____

_____

_____

_____

What activities are most likely to get you upset if they do not go right?

_____

_____

_____

_____

_____

_____

_____

Who are the most likely people to upset you if your meeting with them does not go right?

_____

_____

_____

_____

_____

Chapter 3

Stick with Primary Feelings

One of the ways that you can control yourself is to understand how your emotional reactions drive your thoughts and behaviors. The following exercises will help you understand how your emotions build on each other and become distorted and lead to bad thoughts and behavior.

The good news is that with some awareness and training, you will discover that you have primary and secondary emotions. Primary emotions are those that include shock and surprise. Secondary emotions include jealousy and anger. Sticking with the primary emotions leads to your being more honest with yourself and puts you in a better position to handle the situation appropriately. To stick with primary emotions, you first must identify them and then act on them. The following examples will help you clarify what your primary emotions are.

Emotional Awareness Situations

Below are three different scenarios. Read each one of these situations and then answer the questions that follow.

Fred and His Date

Fred and his first-time date go with another couple (friends he has known for years) to a local night club on the weekend. As Fred is sipping his glass of draft, he notices his new date is making eye contact and smiling with another fellow who is sitting with a group of guys at a table at the far end of the night club. A few moments later, she tells Fred that she must go to the bathroom. When she returns from the bathroom, she takes the long way around the inside of the night club and leans over the other men's table, smiling, and carries on a rather long conversation with the guy with whom she had made eye contact, as well as with the other fellows at that table. Fred's friend, Tom (who is sitting with him at the table) leans over and asks Fred, "What the hell is going on over there? You're looking pretty bad, my friend. She's making you look pathetic!" A few moments after that remark, she returns to the table. She seems in a very happy mood.

If you were Fred

(a) What would you think?

_____

_____

_____

_____

_____

(b) How would you feel?

_____

_____

_____

_____

_____

(c) Most likely, what would you do?

_____

_____

_____

_____

_____

Steve the Volleyball Pro

Steve plays volleyball in the men's pick up league every Wednesday night at the YMCA. The level of competition is pretty high. Name calling sometimes occurs because the title and overall prize winners are awarded a trophy and cash.

During a fairly intense game, Steve jumped to get a shot, missed the shot, and fell into the net. The left bar that held the net up came undone and fell over, causing a prolonged break in the action. One of Steve's coworkers happened to be playing on the opposite team. Seeing that Steve was apparently embarrassed about knocking over the net, his coworker yelled across the gym to him, "Hey, Stevie boy! Did you forget that you had two left feet? You're lucky to be able to walk over to get the ball, let alone fly over! Well, Steve what do you have to say about that! Stevie, I'm talking to you!"

If you were Steve at that moment

(a) What would you think?

_____

_____

_____

_____

_____

_____

(b) How would you feel?

_____

_____

_____

_____

_____

(c) Most likely, what would you do?

_____

_____

_____

_____

_____

Jerry's Steak

Jerry has just received parole and is living in a halfway house. According to the rules, he must buy his own food and store it in the community refrigerator. He bought himself a steak and put it in the refrigerator at 1:30 in the afternoon. Today is Jerry's birthday. You guessed it! When he returned to the halfway house with his favorite soft drink and all the necessary stuff to go along with his steak (baked potato, sour cream, bacon bits, and barbecue sauce), his steak was not in the refrigerator. He heard voices in the TV room. As he approached the room, he saw a new house resident sitting down with a plate in front of him finishing off his steak.

If you were Jerry

(a) What would you think?

_____

_____

_____

_____

_____

_____

(b) How would you feel?

_____

_____

_____

_____

_____

_____

(c) Most likely, what would you do?

_____

_____

_____

_____

_____

_____

_____

Emotional Awareness Scenarios Part 2

An important point to be made here is that in each of the scenarios, and often in your own life, you probably did not get angry right away. You probably felt some other emotions first. These first emotions are your primary emotions. They include: shock, surprise, confusion, insecurity, shame, vulnerability, and powerlessness. Your secondary emotions are reactions to the first set of emotions or feelings. They include anger, outrage, jealousy, hate, and resentfulness. The following exercise is very similar to the one you just finished but with this important difference: try to identify what your primary and secondary feelings would be.

In this exercise, read the three examples below. At the end of each example, fill in what you consider to be your primary and secondary feelings as if you were the person in that situation.

Tim and the Blonde Hair

Tim attended an office party. His wife could not go due to illness, so he went alone. During the party, an obviously drunk new employee stumbled and fell into Tim's arms while he was sitting next to his boss. "You are cute" she slurred kissing him before she staggered away. When Tim came home, his wife was sitting at the kitchen table waiting for him. She told him that she had been tipped off that he was necking with a blonde at the party. She saw a smudge of lipstick on his cheek and slowly pulled two strands of blonde hair off his shoulder. "You stinking bastard," was all he heard before feeling the sting of a slap across his face.

If you were Tim, your primary and secondary feelings in this situation would be

Primary feelings _____

_____

_____

Secondary feelings _____

_____

_____

Brad and the Parole Officer

Traditionally, Brad never has experienced any difficulties with his parole officers. As someone who wrote bad checks, he had been involved with three parole officers in the past. His new parole officer, however, is a different story. He phoned immediately upon Brad's release and ordered him to be in his office by 10:00 A.M. or else he said Brad would be sent back to prison so fast it would make his head spin. When he first met with the parole officer, the parole officer told him "I don't take any crap from slime like you. You should have been locked up and the key thrown away." Then, the parole officer said, "I will tell you when to speak, but until then, shut up and listen and learn from me."

If you were Brad, your primary and secondary feelings in this situation would be

Primary feelings _____

_____

_____

Secondary feelings _____

_____

_____

Mike's Camping Trip

Mike was the last person to join the camping trip in the woods. He did not think anything of the fact that he drove the six guys in his van to the camp site. He was just happy to have been invited as part of the group. He was a little bothered that everyone placed their food together to be divided and shared by all. He was more upset that he had to stay back and cook the steaks on the second day while the others took his van and went out on a scouting mission on the back roads. When they returned, he saw scratches and dents on the side of his van. At that point, it became clear to him: he was a patsy! He was being used by the others for transportation, for mooching off his good food (steak, bacon, and eggs), while they only contributed beans, wieners, and soup. Further, they just had used his van as an off-road all-terrain vehicle.

If you were Mike, your primary and secondary feelings in this situation would be

Primary feelings _____

_____

_____

Secondary feelings _____

_____

_____

Why I Do Not Deal with My Primary Feelings

In this chapter, we talked about primary and secondary feelings. List the reasons why you may not deal with your primary feelings as much as you should.

_____

_____

_____

_____

_____

_____

_____

_____

_____

Chapter 4

Misperceptions, Sabotage, and Primary Feelings

The Channel Demon

Sandy is at a female halfway house. She is in the living room watching a movie on TV. She has watched the first hour and a half of a two-hour movie when two other female residents enter the room and sit down. One asks the other what she would like to watch on TV, totally ignoring Sandy. The second one answers, "Let's watch the game show on Channel 5." The first woman picks up the remote and clicks it over to Channel 5.

Sandy may think, "That b_ _ _ _! She did that on purpose! She may feel outraged or furious. She is trying to make me look bad—like a jerk! I'll show her!" Sandy's behavior is to call her a b_ _ _ _, grab the remote out of her hand, and flick it back to her movie.

Given the same situation as Sandy's, another person, Mary thinks, "Why did she do that? Didn't she realize I was watching a movie?" Mary feels irritated. She feels as if she were given little or no respect by the woman who turned the channel. Mary's behavior is to tap the woman on the shoulder, look her straight in the eye, and calmly and assertively indicate that she was watching a movie and expects that she will be able to watch it until it finishes half an hour from now.

Misperceptions

In this example of the channel demon, we saw what objectively happened in that situation. What objectively happens and our perceptions are two different issues. In the case of Sandy, for example, she may not have realized that it was a darkened room. The room was quite large and the two ladies, in fact, might not have seen her. Sandy, however, immediately interpreted the event (or perceived the situation) as if they had seen her and purposely ignored her!

In the case of Mary, she gave them the benefit of the doubt. Before overreacting on false perceptions, she chose to state her position assertively in a nondefensive fashion to see if the ladies purposely were ignoring her or were committing an "honest" mistake.

When people are generally at ease with themselves and are fairly relaxed, they are much more willing to interpret or perceive an event (especially a negative event) as being an honest mistake. People are much more patient and forgiving in these situations. Sometimes individuals have a hard day when nothing seems to go right. On these days, even an honest accident or mistake may be interpreted or perceived as a purposeful, hurtful action.

Sabotaging Thoughts

When individuals make a misperception or misinterpretation of somebody else's actions, they tend to experience sabotaging thoughts. In the TV example, Sandy perceived what objectively happened (ladies coming into a room that was darkened and changing the channel on the television set) and perceived that it was done on purpose. This allowed a series of sabotaging thoughts to run through her head. Some of these thoughts may have been the following: They cannot treat me like this. I'll show them! Who the hell do they think they are? They are always picking on me. Well, that's the straw that broke the camel's back! And now, I'm going to get even! There is no middle ground here—no room for negotiation. It is simply, I am right and they are wrong. They are going to pay!

Sabotaging thoughts only fuel your inappropriate feelings! They tend to justify your being abusive or, in some cases, violent. They make you feel justified in your actions (behavior). This is because your sabotaging thoughts have led you to feel justified in whatever action you are about to take.

In Mary's case, she did not allow sabotaging thoughts to enter into her interpretation of the situation. She was concerned, but left it at that. She allowed the other people the benefit of the doubt until she could gather all of the facts to determine if they, in fact, had changed the channel on purpose. If she had assertively asked the question and found out that they, in fact, were being purposely mean or demeaning to her, at that point she may have become angry. But she was certainly not "jumping the gun" as Sandy was. When Mary pointed out that she was there first, that there was only thirty minutes left of the movie, and that they could have the TV afterwards, they obliged her.

The scenario could have turned out differently. When she tried to reason with them, they could have laughed at her, told her they were not interested in the movie, and told her to take a walk. In that instance, Mary would have a decision to make about the following options:

A. She could try further negotiation.

B. She could indicate that she was going to minimize their viewing pleasure by heckling.

C. She could challenge them and end up fighting them.

D. She could complain to a staff member.

E. She wisely could decide that since there were two of them, and they would not back down, that she should walk away knowing that you cannot win every situation.

There are pluses and minuses with each choice. List the pluses and minuses for each choice.

pluses:

A. _____

B. _____

C. _____

D. _____

E. _____

minuses:

A. _____

B. _____

C. _____

D. _____

E. _____

If Mary is returning to the street and is under the watchful eye of her parole officer or halfway house counselor, she would be wise to choose E and walk away. Choice C is a return ticket to prison.

Primary and Secondary Feelings

Given the previous situation, most people would feel that Sandy became angry when she believed the other two ladies were ignoring her and changing the channel. This is only partially true. Sandy's anger was only a "secondary" feeling. Her "primary" feelings could have been embarrassment, shock, confusion, emotional hurt, and so forth.

It is worth noting that men might have even more difficulty than women in handling this situation. Many men have been raised in environments that call for them to engage in male macho posturing; to be verbally and physically intimidating; and not to show primary feelings of being hurt or embarrassed. Instead, they are encouraged to react quickly in an aggressive fashion. The actors in action adventure movies are our heroes. The enforcers on a sports team gain our attention and sometimes our respect. Although, the times are changing, many males now are socialized not to lash out but to settle issues verbally. This option avoids the type of aggressive confrontation that could lead to incarceration.

Yet, neither women nor men like experiencing primary feelings. This occurs because we have little or no appropriate way to express these feelings. They are uncomfortable feelings. We do not find it socially acceptable, for example, to break down and cry if we feel emotional hurt. We do not like to admit that we are feeling helpless or insecure, or afraid of losing someone. Quite often, we channel our primary feelings into secondary feelings because, with our secondary feelings, we have a much wider means of displaying these feelings. In the above example, Sandy's primary feelings turned to anger, and she reacted the way she normally would react when she becomes angry.

In Mary's case, her primary feelings were likely that of surprise and possibly some emotional hurt. She channeled these into an assertive problem-solving behavior instead of reacting with angry behaviors.

Think of what can you do to clear up the situations so they are not as maddening and filled with anger for everybody. There are a number of things you can do.

1. You can try to stick with your primary feelings (confusion, uncertainty, shock, insecurity, and so forth) and try to work with the situation based on these feelings. You must try to think of various thoughts and behaviors that directly relate to your primary feelings.

2. You can be honest. There is no need to role play or to make threats that you could not carry through or that, if you did carry through, would get you back behind bars.

3. You can try to communicate. Ask the other person what the problem is . . . without making threats.

4. You can use a lot of statements such as "I am feeling a little insecure, confused, or jealous over what I just saw."

5. Do not assume anything! You probably have heard that the word "assume" simply results in from making an ass (out of) u (and) me.

Fred and His Date—Part 2

Now we will return to Fred. Remember, his girlfriend just came back to his table. Here is an example of the wrong way to do things.

Fred: What the hell do you think you are doing! You better come straight with me and tell me what is going on, and it better be damn good!

Girlfriend: What are you talking about?

Fred: You know damn well what I'm talking about! I ought to punch you out right here and now for making me look stupid!

Girlfriend: I don't know what you are talking about, and you do not need any help from me to look stupid!

Fred: (feeling a little lost now in the conversation but still angry) Look, you owe me an explanation!

Girlfriend: I don't owe you anything. You don't own me! I can do what I want when I want.

Fred: (now extremely angry) I'll teach you who's boss!

Is this a little far fetched? This is an example of a likely set of consequences for people who tend to be very angry. Now, if only Fred had stayed with his "primary" feelings, maybe everything would have happened in the following manner.

Fred: Look, I've got to talk to you about something very important.

Girlfriend: Yes, what is it?

Fred: I'm very confused about what I just saw. It seemed to me as if you were having a great time with that table of guys over there. I've got to admit I'm feeling jealous. Help me clear up this confusion.

Girlfriend: Oh, I'm sorry you were feeling that way. That's just my cousin, Jack, from out of town. He and some buddies are here to see the concert tomorrow night. Don't worry, I think you're awesome.

Both laugh and hug each other.

Yes, maybe this situation was a bit too sugar coated. But the general intent still holds. By sticking with your primary feelings, you can tend to go further towards defusing a situation and working things out rather than confronting that other person, getting his or her back up against the wall and having both of you become angry at the very least, and perhaps even aggressive.

Now comes the homework.

Here are some homework assignments for you to complete. Keep up the good work and remember to be honest in what you are writing. It is for your benefit! Write down a few situations in which you were angry. Describe what the situation was, and what your primary feelings were. Now, we understand that you likely became angry in that situation and we want to know what you actually did in that event. But we want you also to make an attempt to try to work out how you could have resolved that angry situation by sticking with your primary feelings. Write down how you think you could have acted on the following steps: sticking with primary feelings; being honest; communicating with the other person; and using "I" statements).

The Angry Situation/Primary Feeling Exercise 1

Describe the situation that made you feel angry.

_____

_____

_____

_____

_____

_____

What were your primary feelings?

_____

_____

_____

What did you actually do in that situation when you became angry?

_____

_____

_____

_____

_____

_____

How could you have stayed with your "primary feelings" and handled the situation better?

_____

_____

_____

_____

_____

The Angry Situation/Primary Feeling Exercise 2

Describe the situation that made you feel angry.

_____

_____

_____

_____

_____

_____

_____

_____

What were your primary feelings?

_____

_____

_____

What did you actually do in that situation when you became angry?
How could you have stayed with your "primary feelings" and handled
the situation better?

_____

_____

_____

_____

_____

The Angry Situation/Primary Feeling Exercise 3

Describe the situation that made you feel angry.

_____

_____

_____

_____

_____

_____

_____

_____

What were your primary feelings?

_____

_____

_____

What did you actually do in that situation when you became angry?

_____

_____

_____

_____

How could you have stayed with your "primary feelings" and handled the situation better?

_____

_____

_____

_____

Chapter 5

A Slice of Relapse: Anger Prevention

Relapse prevention helps people manage their troubling thoughts, feelings, and behaviors. Relapse prevention assists people in identifying the thoughts, feelings, and behaviors that individuals have just before their negative behavior occurs. Relapse prevention is accomplished by the individual either alone or with the help, support, and monitoring by a counselor, a family member, and/or friends.

The majority of people who attended rehabilitation programs for substance abuse often returned to substance abuse within a short time. Not all of the treatment programs are ineffective, but a vast majority of them have high "failure" rates. This is because a piece of the treatment puzzle is missing. What the majority of programs lacked was a systematic method of performing a personalized analysis of thoughts, feelings, and behaviors.

This relapse prevention method was the missing piece of the puzzle, and this method of analysis now helps each participant from returning to their problem behavior. By applying it, they now can avoid relapsing back into taking drugs, drinking, or whatever their problem may be. Relapse prevention has had wide application for helping individuals with problems of compulsive gambling, abusing of alcohol and drugs, overeating, and engaging in family violence. Relapse prevention also is suitable for managing your anger.

Presently, we are not concerned with all of the complex processes involved with relapse prevention. Here, we only are looking at the concepts of "lapses" and "identification of risk." Therefore, this manual is intended to show those who go through it the general idea of relapse prevention.

Risky Business and Other Bad Business Dealings

Okay, you are over halfway to the finish line! You are doing great. The fact that you still are reading this manual shows your motivation and commitment to make a change for the positive.

The next step towards achieving your goal of being able to manage your anger is to identify high risk material. Do the following "Risky Business" exercises. They are fairly simple exercises but ones that will take a lot of time and effort for you to complete in the right way. They ask you to identify risky thoughts, feelings, behaviors, persons, and places that put you at the greatest risk for being aggressive. Here is an example of Frank.

Frank thinks that people are out to get him, especially when he is feeling down.

Lately, Frank has been down on his luck. His boss is giving him a rough time at work, and he is having money problems. Frank feels helpless and unable to cope with the situation as it stands right now in his life. His behavior or answer to it all is to drink.

Frank drinks because he feels like a mouse when he is sober. He thinks that people are not willing to have conversations with him. They overlook him. He feels unwanted. The more he feels like this, the more he drinks.

Frank thinks what he would really like to do is to impress other people. If he impressed others, then he would feel important—worthy of their attention. His behavior is to spend money foolishly to buy other people drinks at the bar.

Frank's routine runs on the following schedule. On Monday morning, Frank has a hangover. He has to go to work, but because of the pressures, he drinks during the lunch hour. After lunch, partly due to the fact that he has been drinking, he does a sloppy job. He goes to the bar with his "buddies" (buddies because he pays for the drinks so they are willing to go with him), and plays pool with them. Because of the fact that he knows he has to pay for the drinks to have these fellows hang around, and he has done sloppy job at work, he usually gets in a foul mood. Because he is drinking, he gets much "louder" than the others. His pool-playing ability is getting progressively worse because he is drunk. He becomes upset that he is losing games. He becomes aggressive and maybe fights with the others. He spends all his money buying drinks for himself and his "buddies" and goes home to a cold supper. Following the partially eaten cold supper, he gets into a major argument with his wife and falls asleep on the couch. That, unfortunately, is Frank's life.

It is a pretty easy exercise to pick out Frank's risky thoughts, feelings, behaviors, persons, and places. They already have been outlined for you.

His risky thoughts are the following: They are out to get me, especially when I am down! He thinks he has to impress other people. He even may think that his wife does not want him around (that is true especially when he is drinking and abusive towards her).

Frank's risky feelings also include the feelings of being helpless and unable to cope with his day-to-day life; feeling like a "mouse"; and feeling that he has to have friends around to make him feel important.

Frank's risky behaviors are drinking at work; drinking, in general; spending money foolishly to "buy" friends; and getting into arguments and fights with others.

Obviously, his risky places include the bar scene. Risky people are those fellows who only will be around him as long as he is "buying."

He repeats the same thoughts, feelings, and behaviors several times a week. Therefore, it is easy to pick out his risky business.

Now comes the hard part. You guessed it! In the next section, you will be asked to write down your "risky" business. Remember, you must take the necessary time and effort to fill this out fully. Although the explanation for relapse prevention is the same for everyone, the answers you are filling in apply only to you.

My Risky Business

In the *Cage Your Rage* workbook, you wrote down, specifically in your case, some of the thoughts, body signs, situations, and behaviors that indicated to you that you were becoming angry. Because the next part to the puzzle relies on this, a quick review is in order:

To remind you, when you looked over many of your aggressive outbursts, there were early warning signs that happened just before you became aggressive or abusive. You considered those early warning signs under the categories of thoughts, feelings, and behaviors that put you at risk of getting into another anger cycle.

Thoughts

Thoughts really start the ball rolling towards your acting out in an aggressive or abusive way. Depending on what type of mood you are in, that fellow who you do not know who accidentally spills coffee on you at the food court might have done it by "accident." If you were in a bad mood, you would tend to perceive it as happening on purpose. Each of those particular thoughts would affect your feelings, resulting interpretation, and eventually your behavior. Pay special attention to the cues or warning signs that you are becoming angry.

Listed below are some "typical" thoughts that people say to themselves that build their anger:

Who does he think he is?

He did that on purpose!

You just wait!

He deserves to be hurt for making me look bad!

He's not going to get away with this!

In the spaces provided below, list eight typical thoughts that you can remember thinking while you were angry. These are those particular thoughts that you often think. They are the ones you have to start working on changing. So, if possible, list the ones that you usually have when you are becoming angry. If not, however, list the ones that you can remember from the last few times that you were angry. For the moment, ignore the space left for the Coping Thoughts.

Common Thoughts that Feed My Anger

Risky Thoughts   Coping Thoughts

1. _____   : _____

2. _____   : _____

3. _____   : _____

4. _____   : _____

5. _____   : _____

6. _____   : _____

7. _____   : _____

8. _____   : _____

You are doing a great job! But, it is too soon to slow down now!

Feelings

We already have discussed how your primary feelings usually are not dealt with and, instead, you move onto secondary feelings such as anger. In anger, you feel that you have a whole range of well-tested behaviors, which you may use to express yourself.

Some of the "primary" feelings that you may experience include:

Confusion

Insecurity

Helplessness

Some "secondary" feelings include:

Jealousy

Embarrassment

Frustration

Go ahead, list, as they apply to you, several feelings that usually feed your anger. Again, for right now, ignore the Coping Thoughts on the right.

Common Feelings that Feed My Anger

Risky Thoughts and Feelings   Coping Thoughts

1. _____ : _____

2. _____ : _____

3. _____ : _____

4. _____ : _____

5. _____ : _____

6. _____ : _____

7. _____ : _____

8. _____ : _____

Behaviors

Behaviors are extremely important in the circle of anger and aggression. No matter how mad you become or how much you think that you should be aggressive towards another individual, it is what you actually do, or the action that you take (in the form of a behavior) that causes damage. Some people actually "do" nothing. They store up their anger and then wind up exploding or unloading the anger onto somebody else. They may destroy cars, chairs, TVs, and other things. It may take some people a long time, holding in all different types of hurt, until they finally explode. There are other people who tend to be very aggressive. They talk loudly, point fingers, demand to have things their own way, actually "defy" the other person to question or even talk back to them. It is important for you to be able to identify what common behaviors you exhibit as a result of becoming angry. Some of the examples below are typical:

- abusing alcohol or drugs

- pacing around a room

- raising your voice

- withdrawing from other people and brooding in a corner somewhere

- breaking into a sweat

- knotting in your stomach

- staring at the person with whom you are becoming angry

- having a dry mouth

- shaking or trembling

In the spaces on the next page, list several behaviors that you experience just before you become angry. For right now, leave the Coping Thoughts column blank.

Common Behaviors that Feed my Anger

Risky Thoughts and Behaviors   Coping Thoughts

1. _____ : _____

2. _____ : _____

3. _____ : _____

4. _____ : _____

5. _____ : _____

6. _____ : _____

Situations

There are many common situations or places that people can list that cause them to become angry. Some of these are as follows:

- bar or pool hall
- in-laws visiting the house for the weekend of a special event
- debt collectors or buddies asking for money back that they had loaned you
- not having enough money for cigarettes, lunches at work

Think about it. Be honest with yourself. Provide several examples on the next page that make you angry. Again, skip the column of Coping Thoughts on the right.

Common Situations in Which I Become Angry

Risky Places or Situations	Coping Thoughts
1.	:
2.	:
3.	:
4.	:
5.	:

People With Whom You Get Angry

In addition to having common body signs, "mind" signs of anger, and situations in which you typically may become angry, you may find that there are certain types of people with whom you get angry. For example, some people get angry with their wife or girlfriend quite often. It may be your in-laws, maybe the neighbor's dog who leaves "gifts" on your lawn, and so forth. It is important for you to become aware of these people, as well. Provide several examples of people with whom you get angry.

Again, enter nothing in the Coping Thoughts column.

People Who Anger Me

Risky Persons	Coping Thoughts
1.	:
2.	:
3.	:
4.	:

Coping Strategies

You may have noticed that in completing the previous risky business questions, information spaces were left for you to write appropriate coping strategies. These strategies involve thinking appropriate thoughts. Remember, the reason you are reading this book is because you have problems with your present lifestyle—whether it is your thoughts, feelings, behaviors, places, or persons—things are not working out well for you. And, some things have to change! That is why you have to develop a new game plan. This new game plan will provide your coping side of the risky business list. Go back to the lists, review them, and make any changes where you think it is necessary. Take a break from this book for a while before moving on to the next concept.

Despite our best efforts at trying to make positive change, we frequently undermine ourselves. For example, you may be trying to cut down on the number of arguments that you have with your partner (boyfriend/girlfriend, common law, spouse, and so forth). You may have gotten into a very dirty name-calling contest that resulted in harsh feelings for long periods of time. Therefore, you made a resolution to try not to argue any more. Things actually may go fine for you for a few weeks, but then you have a major blow-out!

When this blow-out occurs, you really feel defeated. You put so much time and effort into this venture you were hoping that things would change. But, obviously, this does not seem to be the way that this is going to be. You are doomed to a life of fighting with your partner—at least verbally and maybe even physically. You might just as well accept your fate because you are doomed to argue at the drop of a hat. Wait. All of this is silly! All of this is untrue! You are undermining or sabotaging yourself!

Just because you had one argument in the last month does not mean that your efforts all should be thrown out. You might have argued with your partner on an average of two or three times a week before. Now that you have had one argument in the last month, don't you see any positive changes? Come on! You probably have made a tremendous amount of progress. Why not look at the positive side of things! Do not be so down on yourself.

Unfortunately, we usually view life from this negative perspective. If you wrote a poem or drew a picture, and nine people gave you compliments on it, but one person criticized it, guess what you would dwell upon—the one negative comment! Why be concerned with that one negative response when nine people—a full 90 percent of the responses—were favorable? Human nature makes us look at a glass and say it is half empty rather than half full. To achieve success in this program, you can learn to overcome that type of thinking. By reading this book up to this point, you have to put a lot of time and effort into managing your anger and aggression. So, the next step is this: Do not "beat up on yourself"!

Here is one of the last bits of the relapse-prevention information that we are covering—sabotaging business.

Sabotaging Business

When you have slipped or "messed up," you often have sabotaging thoughts, feelings, and behaviors. These thoughts and feelings make you want to give up and "throw in the towel." By identifying them, you are well on your way to managing your aggression and abuse!

Before you start your next assignment, here is an example to follow. We return to Frank and his situation. He often would drink at work because he felt like a mouse. He had sloppy work habits and would go to the bar with his so called "buddies" after work and spend what little money he had. He would play pool and get into arguments and possibly into fights. He would return home only to eat a cold supper and prepare for an evening of arguing with his wife. The arguments usually resulted in his sleeping on the couch, and waking up the next morning with a hangover. He would return to work and live the cycle over and over again. Assume for a minute that Frank read through this manual and actually had made some positive changes in his life. He "went" on the wagon and stopped drinking. He stopped trying to impress other people. He stopped arguing with other people. He felt confident at work.

One day his boss called him into the office and onto the mat for his sloppy work performance over the last six months. The boss failed to mention that Frank has seemed to improve over the last two months. Frank panics and his behavior is to run to the bar and drink over the noon hour.

He thinks to himself: my new way of behaving did not work for me. I have thrown it all away; it didn't work! He sabotages his last two months of good behavior by thinking that he only feels powerful and confident when he has had a number of drinks. His behavior is to drink the third and fourth and fifth beer. He continues to think "I'm a loser!" He feels that he cannot cope without the alcohol. He feels angry at himself and his behavior is to start playing pool with whomever is at the bar.

Now that you have heard and read about the concepts and have an example of poor Frank and his dilemmas, apply the material to yourself. Fill out the following chart based on your own life. Good luck. Nobody said it was going to be easy.

Sabotaging Thoughts   Coping Thoughts

_____ : _____

_____ : _____

_____ : _____

_____ : _____

Sabotaging Feelings   Coping Thoughts

_____ : _____

_____ : _____

_____ : _____

_____ : _____

Sabotaging Behaviors   Coping Thoughts

_____ : _____

_____ : _____

_____ : _____

_____ : _____

Sabotaging Persons	Coping Thoughts
	:
	:
	:
	:

Sabotaging Places	Coping Thoughts
	:
	:
	:
	:

Now, go back to the "Coping Thoughts" columns that you left blank in this chapter. Add practical coping thoughts that will help you deal with each of these situations.

Chapter 6

Relapse Prevention Games: Practice Makes Perfect

Practice Scenarios

Below are real life events that may happen to you. Imagine yourself in each situation. Think about what your reactions would be if each of these things actually happened to you. After reading each one, write down your thoughts, feelings, and behaviors. In your thoughts, try to come up with your primary and secondary thoughts. Your primary thoughts often reflect your worries, your concerns, and your insecurities. Your secondary thoughts come out as a reaction to those primary thoughts. They might be quite negative and destructive. Your feelings come from the thoughts, and when the primary thoughts are about how insecure and hurt you are, you want to lash out and hurt back.

Given those thoughts and feelings, you can look at what your behaviors would be if you gave into your worst thoughts and feelings and what they would be if you tried to think about the best way to react to this situation. Following your reactions are some suggestions of things that you might have thought, felt, or done. There are no real "right" answers, and maybe you can do better than the suggested answers that follow each example. Before you read the suggested answers, fill out your responses. Then, rate yourself on how close you are to the suggestions out of a possible score of three. Give yourself 1 if you are way off, 2 for not bad, and 3 for excellent—you should be a counselor!

1. Your kids have a chip on their shoulder against you because you were in prison. You spent all that time away from them. They are angry at you. They know that they can "get at you" by not giving you respect. You are especially upset with your daughter. You do not like the direction she is taking. She has rough friends. Some of her friends use drugs. She is staying out later and later. Today, when you tried to talk to her about the direction she is headed in, she shouted at you, got angry, and would not listen. She calls you a "jail bird" and "a loser." She said, "What do you know, you screwup?"

What are your thoughts?

_____

_____

_____

_____

_____

What do you feel?

_____

_____

_____

_____

_____

What are your behaviors?

_____

_____

_____

_____

_____

Ideally, what should your behaviors be?

_____

_____

_____

_____

_____

Answer check:

Primary Thoughts

I am concerned about my daughter.

I'm no good as a parent.

Geez, I really screwed up this family.

They are not respecting me.

They do not love me.

I am irrelevant to them.

They do not care about me.

They are rejecting me.

Secondary Thoughts

My own kid is mean, stupid, and rejecting. I am only trying to help.

It is unnatural for a child to hate her parents. I will show her who is boss.

I'm her father, damn it! She has to show me respect!

Emotions (Feelings):

From primary thoughts: frustration, depression, panic, worry, upset, inadequacy, rejection

From secondary thoughts: strong anger, hate, disgust, helplessness

Behaviors:

From primary thoughts and feelings: falling silent, ignoring daughter, pouting

From secondary thoughts and feelings: lashing out in anger, "You rotten little _ _ _ _ _ !," stomping away angry, and saying "I give up."

Ideally, what you would do:

You might face her calmly and say: "I know you do not respect me, but I have had a lot of experience in life." She will have all kinds of annoying, lippy answers, but control yourself, and you will start to get through to her about your worries concerning her. If you attack her from your anger, she will retreat further into her so-called friends. If you can talk to her, you can start to bring her around. It may be more difficult than you think because you expect children to respect their parents and every time she shows disrespect, you almost could lose it, but hang in there!

You are talking to her to

(1) find out what she thinks is good and bad. You might be surprised about how many things on which you agree.

(2) find a way to show the bad elements in her friends to weaken their hold on her.

(3) show her that you and your judgment can be trusted.

There is no magic, instant miracle cure but, over time, things will get better than if you drive her away with anger or give up on her.

Give yourself a score from 1 to 3 on how well you answered on situation # 1:_____

Remember, a score of 1 means you were off on the wrong track; a score of 2 indicates you are doing okay on this situation, and a score of 3 means excellent—you should be a counselor!

2. You and your girlfriend do not live together, but you expect to come over when you are free to hang out, eat dinner, and stay over. Generally, you get on pretty well, but you also have your little troubles. Lately, you have a few small issues, but every couple does. Today, you call her and she says she has relatives driving in this afternoon. She is going to feed them dinner, and since she has plenty of room, they are going to stay overnight. She does not mention inviting you. Immediately, you get the idea that you are not welcome. She complains about how busy work is, how she will have to work late, and then how she will have to put together a nice dinner for them. Because there is still no invitation for you for the dinner, you think she picks up on your disappointment. At the end of the conversation, she says to meet her for a quick lunch, but she still has not invited you for dinner or to meet the relatives.

What are your primary and secondary thoughts about this?

_____

_____

_____

_____

_____

_____

How do you feel?

_____

_____

_____

_____

_____

What are your behaviors?

_____

_____

_____

_____

_____

What should your ideal behaviors be?

_____

_____

_____

_____

_____

_____

What are you thinking?

_____

_____

_____

_____

_____

_____

Primary thoughts:

I thought we were made for each other, but she is ashamed to introduce me to her relatives! She thinks I am not good enough!

This shows me how stupid I can be.

She really pulled the rug out from under me this time.

Even though she heard the disappointment in my voice, she still did not invite me.

She just does not care.

Secondary thoughts:

What a _ _ _ _ _!

She is trying to appease me by eating lunch with me. What a manipulator!

There is no #@&%#*$ way I will eat with her.

If that is the way she wants to be, she and her relatives can go &#%@ themselves!

I do not know how she can ever make this up to me.

I won't forget this!

I'll get her back!

Emotions

Primary feelings: hurt, fear, anxiety, depression, surprise, worry, insecurity, vulnerability, stupidity

Secondary feelings: anger, desire for revenge, frustration

What are your behaviors towards her?

From primary thoughts and feelings: withdrawing, being cold, acting tough, hiding feelings. You think: There is no way I am going to have lunch with her!

From secondary thoughts and feelings: Plan revenge, stand her up for dates, avoid her, disappoint her, forget her birthday, give her the cold, silent treatment

Ideally, what you should do:

I will tell her how much this hurts me. I will listen to her side of the story. I will ask her if it is my prison record. Maybe it is. Who knows? Maybe her dad is a minister, or a correctional officer, or her brother is a cop, and our relationship might freak them out right now. Maybe she is so serious about me that she does not want any family pressure to try and divide us. Or maybe she figured that I would not want to come over when they were there. At least, you can find out rather than immediately jumping to the most negative kinds of thoughts.

Give yourself a score from 1 to 3 on how well you answered on situation # 2:_____

Remember, a score of 1 means you were off on the wrong track; a score of 2 indicates you are doing okay on this situation, and a score of 3 means excellent—you should be a counselor!

3.   You have been doing very well at your job. You like the work, and the boss generally is pleased with you. The guy you are working with, however, is a real dip. He complains about the work, has a bad attitude, and is not very good with the customers. The real problem is that, every time the boss comes by, this person starts to order you around or make suggestions about what you should be doing. You know that he is trying to make himself look eager. This bugs you because it is a lie. He hates the job. What is worse is that he is trying to impress the boss by making you look bad! You are so busy working that you do not always see the boss come in, but this person just seems to know. So, today you are cleaning up around some displays and your coworker says "Hey, shouldn't you be looking after that customer? You cannot keep them waiting you know." You look by the counter and see the customer. You look over by the office and there is the boss standing by the door. One second more, and you would have seen the customer and helped him. It is also the coworker's job to serve customers but, again, your coworker has made you look like a fool! You are getting insecure wondering what the boss thinks of you.

What are your primary and secondary thoughts about this?

_____

_____

_____

_____

_____

How do you feel?

_____

_____

_____

_____

_____

What are your behaviors?

_____

_____

_____

_____

_____

What should your ideal behaviors be?

_____

_____

_____

_____

_____

Primary thoughts:

This person is trying to look good by making me look bad.

This person is a real manipulator.

I'm looking pretty foolish. I'm the ex-con. My boss will think badly of me.

Secondary thoughts:

My coworker is a jerk. I could kill that bastard!

Emotions

Primary feelings: anxiety, helplessness, insecurity, worry, upset, embarrassment

Secondary feelings: frustration and anger

Behaviors

Behaviors from primary thoughts and feelings: give up, let the jerk order you around, do not work too hard because you can never impress the boss anyway

Behaviors from secondary thoughts and feelings: be uncooperative, show a bad attitude (especially to the coworker), swear at or threaten the coworker

A more appropriate response would be to:

Face your coworker. Tell him that he is not the boss. Explain that you are concerned about doing a good job and do not need him to say how to do it. Tell him that you know that your boss is pretty smart and will figure out what is happening. When your coworker sees that the manipulation is not working, he might get discouraged and back off. If you can relax a little over the situation, you might be able to come back with a few lines yourself. Try something like "Look, if we work together, we would be able to help the customers faster!"

Give yourself a score from 1 to 3 on how well you answered on situation # 3:_____

Remember, a score of 1 means you were off on the wrong track; a score of 2 indicates you are doing okay on this situation, and a score of 3 means excellent—you should be a counselor!

More Practice Scenarios

4. You are trying to keep out of every kind of trouble with the law so you are driving the speed limit. You look in the rear-view mirror, and some guy in a big-wheeled pickup truck with the stereo so loud you can feel its vibrations is tailgating you. He is trying to make you speed up or get out of the way. The road is a little slippery with slush, and the last thing you want is this jerk ramming you. You cannot pull to the side because of snow. Speeding up is out of the question because you do not want to be pulled over, and also it is slippery enough so you could lose control of the car. Finally, this jerk whips out and passes, gives you the finger, and cuts in so fast that you have to brake. You have to quickly brake again, almost losing control, as he decides to brake quickly to turn into a store parking lot.

What are your primary and secondary thoughts about this?

_____

_____

_____

_____

_____

How do you feel?

_____

_____

_____

_____

_____

What are your behaviors?

_____

_____

_____

_____

_____

_____

What should your ideal behaviors be?

_____

_____

_____

_____

_____

Primary thoughts:

What is this guy doing? This is dangerous.

I am going to get run off the road and hurt.

Secondary thoughts:

The guy is a class A-1 jerk.

I would like to ring his neck, tie him to the front bumper and ram the wall!

Emotions

Primary feelings: fear, confusion, worry

Secondary feelings: anger and frustration

Behaviors from primary thoughts: look for turnoff, get out of the way, speed up

Behaviors from secondary thoughts: get angry, want to kill, approach in the parking lot to yell at and then thump the jerk, and, oops! Back to jail!

What you might try:

You also can turn into the parking lot. You can get the license number and report the guy to the local police department. You might be pleasantly surprised that the police keep records. With enough reports that driver can lose his license.

Give yourself a score from 1 to 3 on how well you answered on situation # 4:_____

Remember, a score of 1 means you were off on the wrong track; a score of 2 indicates you are doing okay on this situation, and a score of 3 means excellent—you should be a counselor!

5. You screwed up before, and that is how you got sent to prison in the first place. Now, you are out. You have completed the programs they had in prison and you have changed. You are not perfect, yet, but you are trying. You are finally an adult and, for the first time, you like yourself! It is just your parents who do not seem to recognize it. They are treating you like a kid. They ask who you are hanging around with. They make judgments on your friends. They get upset if you have a couple of drinks. You did your time! You paid your dues! You are responsible! You have a parole officer on your case. You do not need them always getting so excited over what you do. Every time you get a chance to show you know what you are doing and can handle yourself, they take the opportunity away from you and tell you what you should be doing or not doing. The other day you and your buddies were heading for the lake for a couple of days camping. There was some beer in the truck. Your dad was immediately on your case about drinking and driving. There was no way you were going to drink and drive. Mom was going through her big thing about drugs. You have been clean since you left prison and you do not want to even think of the word "drugs," but they keep reminding you. Whose life is it, anyway? You just wish they would shut up and let you live a normal life.

What are your primary and secondary thoughts about this?

_____

_____

_____

_____

_____

_____

How do you feel?

_____

_____

_____

_____

_____

What are your behaviors?

_____

_____

_____

_____

_____

What should your ideal behaviors be?

_____

_____

_____

_____

_____

Primary thoughts:

My parents do not think I am responsible.

They do not think I know right from wrong.

Secondary thoughts:

They make me mad.

I am not a child.

Emotions

Primary feelings: frustration, upset, embarrassment

Secondary feelings: depression and frustration

Behaviors from primary thoughts and feelings: acting grumpy, pouting, whining about parents being unfair

Behaviors from secondary thoughts and feelings: being uncooperative, avoiding parents, avoiding talking, and avoiding telling them what you do, becoming secretive

What you might try:

Sit them down and tell them that you know they are just trying to keep you out of trouble. Tell them that you did screw up but that you paid for it and really learned from it. They are on your side. They are trying to help. You might give them a role. They could be like your conscience on risky behaviors. You might have to review some of your actions and maybe tell them what you think your risky behaviors are and which ones are not. You might be happy if they watch over you for the more dangerous behaviors and leave you alone for the ones that are not. You have to be honest with yourself too, because they just might be right about some things.

Give yourself a score from 1 to 3 on how well you answered on situation # 5:_____

Remember, a score of 1 means you were off on the wrong track; a score of 2 indicates you are doing okay on this situation; and a score of 3 means excellent—you should be a counselor!

6. You are home. The phone rings. You say "hello." A guy asks for your wife by name and says "Who are you, anyway?" You say "I am her husband, who are you?" He hangs up on you immediately. Your wife has gone out for groceries so you have an hour to sit around and "stew" about this call. You had been in prison for a year and half. Your wife is a good looking woman. She never said anything about another guy. You love her, but you know your prison time took some kind of bite out of your marriage. Your wife comes in with a smile and says "Hi."

What are your primary and secondary thoughts about this?

_____

_____

_____

_____

_____

_____

How do you feel?

_____

_____

_____

_____

_____

_____

What are your behaviors?

_____

_____

_____

_____

_____

_____

What should your ideal behaviors be?

_____

_____

_____

_____

_____

_____

Primary thoughts:

Was my wife fooling around?

How could she look at another guy, especially since I love her so much?

As soon as my back was turned in prison, these hyena pig-bastards start hunting my wife!

I trusted her, how much of a fool have I been?

Secondary thoughts:

I'll nail his balls on the barn door if I ever catch him around here.

Man, if my wife was cheating on me, I will go through the roof!

I will not be responsible for what I do.

Emotions

Primary feelings: insecurity, worry, upset, uncertainty

Secondary feelings: embarrassment and anger

Behaviors from primary thoughts and feelings: whining, shouting at her, calling her a _ _ _ _ _; complaining about her clothes, her makeup, and her hair; ask her who is she dressing up for; wonder why she dressed up when she visited prison

Behaviors from secondary thoughts and feelings: threaten her, her boyfriend if any, watch her every move, start controlling and monitoring her comings and goings

What might be better things to do?

You have to think out your situation. The worst is something could have happened—the best is nothing did. You may never really know for sure either way. You were out of action for a year and half. It was your fault. You do not think she could be angry at you for that, buddy. Well, you are living a fantasy! She might have gotten that anger out in a way that you do not like, and you will never know. But face it, where is she now? She is with you. If you torture her over what you can never really prove one way or the other, you are going to ruin the best relationship you can have. A lot of guys lose their loved ones while in prison. Yours is still with you and loving you! You can ask and you can say how much you would be hurt if she did run around on you and how much you would feel betrayed, but you can only push so far because you are to blame for the prison time!

Give yourself a score from 1 to 3 on how well you answered on situation # 6:_____

Remember, a score of 1 means you were off on the wrong track; a score of 2 indicates you are doing okay on this situation; a score of 3 means excellent—you should be a counselor!

7. A couple of friends say "lets go up to the cabin by the lake." It is warm enough for swimming, taking the canoe out, and doing a little fishing. Back to nature sounds pretty good! You have conditions for your parole, and you check with the friends and say "no drugs." They say fine. You get to the place. You are out in the boat but you can see everybody and their dog is dropping by. Most of the cars are just stopping and then taking off again but enough are staying so a party is going on by the time you return. The place is full of drugs. These guys are supplying the whole lake district! The girls hanging around look underage, and you get this sick feeling that their parents and then the police are going to be here soon. You cannot be here! You ask them for a ride out, but they say, "Hey we are not leaving this party." Your friends betrayed you! You told them you could not be around drugs, but they did not give a _____! It would be a first offense for them, but you have a history, and you are going to be in the biggest trouble.

What are your primary and secondary thoughts about this?

_____

_____

_____

_____

_____

_____

How do you feel?

_____

_____

_____

_____

_____

_____

What are your behaviors?

_____

_____

_____

_____

_____

_____

What should your ideal behaviors be?

_____

_____

_____

_____

_____

_____

Primary thoughts:

I am scared.

I do not want to be a killjoy, but if the police come, I am screwed.

A few years ago, I would have thought this was fun, but now I cannot take the risk.

Secondary thoughts:

Some friends, they betrayed me!

What jerks!

They know that with my record, I will go down big time while they probably will get off.

Emotions

Primary feelings: fear, worry, confusion, and upset

Secondary feelings: nervousness and anger

Behaviors from primary thoughts and feelings: complain about the situation, tell the guys to ditch the stuff and clean up their act and get the underage girls out

Behaviors from secondary thoughts and feelings: yell at friends, threaten and insult them, give up and join the party

What you could do:

Ask again for a ride out. If someone comes by who looks pretty sober, try to get a ride out of the area. Hitchhike back to town if you have to. You cannot be caught in this situation. The discomfort of spending your time getting out of there is better than going back to prison.

Give yourself a score from 1 to 3 on how well you handled situation # 7:_____

Remember, a score of 1 means you were off on the wrong track; a score of 2 indicates you are doing okay on this situation; a score of 3 means excellent—you should be a counselor!

Additional Practice Challenges

8. A buddy moved in with you. You did not know him very well, but he said he needed a place to crash for a few days until he got a job and a place of his own. He has gotten pretty comfortable. He is freeloading off you. He never has any money. He gives you nothing for the rent. He uses your soap and your shampoo. Every once in a while he brings in a little food, but always less than his share. You are suspicious but not sure that he is stealing it. Everything about him is bugging you. When you complain, he says "Yeah man, I will pay you back. Just let me find a job." You got sent home from work early today, and you walked in and the place is reeking with marijuana, and he is in your bed with someone.

What are your primary and secondary thoughts about this?

_____

_____

_____

_____

_____

_____

How do you feel?

_____

_____

_____

_____

_____

_____

What are your behaviors?

_____

_____

_____

_____

_____

_____

What should your ideal behaviors be?

_____

_____

_____

_____

_____

_____

Primary thoughts:

This guy is using me.

He is just a loser.

Secondary thoughts:

I have to dump this bum if I am ever going get straightened out.

Emotions

Primary feelings: disgust

Secondary feelings: frustration and anger

Behaviors from primary thoughts and feelings: yell at the guy, call him down, "You loser!"

Behaviors from secondary thoughts and feelings: pack his stuff and throw it out the door

What you could do:

Well, this time you were right—only do not yell! Tell him to pack his own stuff and get out or if he is too big, you are packing and you are out of there! The guy is a leech and he will only bring you down. Some cases are hopeless, so cut your losses now.

Give yourself a score from 1 to 3 on how well you answered on situation # 8:_____

Remember, a score of 1 means you were off on the wrong track; a score of 2 indicates you are doing okay on this situation; and a score of 3 means excellent—you should be a counselor!

9. Every time the family gets together, your cousin brings up your record. He seems to do it every chance he gets. You enjoy being with the family except for this guy. He will not leave you alone. On the beach last week he said, loud enough for everyone to hear, "I bet you do not see tans like that in prison." Before that, your dad was talking about a plane trip and he says "Boy, I bet jailbirds wish they could fly." Two nights ago he, your aunt, your mom and dad, and you were walking past some clubs and your cousin said, "Why don't you walk down the alley to remind you of what it is like behind bars." Tonight, everyone is laughing and joking around at dinner and you are laughing too. Your cousin shouts "Hey everybody, I will bet the jailbird did not laugh like this when he was in his cage."

What are your primary and secondary thoughts about this?

_____

_____

_____

_____

_____

_____

How do you feel?

_____

_____

_____

_____

_____

_____

What are your behaviors?

_____

_____

_____

_____

_____

What should your ideal behaviors be?

_____

_____

_____

_____

_____

_____

Primary thoughts:

I feel so ashamed in front of my family.

I do not need my past thrown in my face every time we get together.

Man, why does my cousin always embarrass me?

Why doesn't he leave it alone?

Secondary thoughts:

My cousin is causing a lot of tension.

I would love to get him like he is getting me.

I would like to kill the &%$$#@ !

I want revenge!

Emotions

Primary feelings: shame, embarrassment, anxiety, depression

Secondary feelings: anger and hate

Behaviors from primary thoughts: sulk, stop enjoying yourself, retreat away from the situation

Behaviors from secondary thoughts: have an angry outburst, punch the guy

What you could do:

Try to figure out why your cousin is doing this. Maybe he is genuinely ashamed of your being in the family. If the majority of the family supports you, then he has to be told by a family member that his behavior is way over the line, and he just has to stop it. Maybe your cousin is jealous because you get more attention than he thinks you deserve. Take him aside, with a third person from the family, and ask him what the problem is. Tell him how he is spoiling good times for everyone by this constant harping. Give him the chance to explain himself and see what you agree or disagree about.

Give yourself a score from 1 to 3 on how well you answered on situation # 9:_____

A score of 1 means you were off on the wrong track; a score of 2 indicates you are doing okay on this situation; a score of 3 means excellent—you should be a counselor!

10. You did it now! Those video lottery machines really have been getting to your wallet. You just gambled away your beer and lunch money for the week. You are not feeling too good about that when a car pulls up beside you. It is your landlord. He says the first of the month is coming up and he needs the rent exactly on that day. He reminds you that you were three days late a couple of months ago and one day late last month.

What are your primary and secondary thoughts about this?

_____

_____

_____

_____

_____

_____

How do you feel?

_____

_____

_____

_____

_____

_____

What are your behaviors?

_____

_____

_____

_____

_____

_____

What should your ideal behaviors be?

_____

_____

_____

_____

_____

_____

Primary thoughts:

I have got to leave those gambling machines alone.

I have lost my money!

I do not know what I am going to do for money for the next few days.

Playing these things is real risky behavior.

Mostly, I lose and even when I win, it does not take me long to lose it again!

Now, the landlord is reminding me about money!

I have to have a roof over my head.

Secondary thoughts:

I am really pissed off at myself, my own stupidity, the store owners, the gambling machine owners, and the government for allowing those damn machines.

The landlord pisses me off! He is a bloody vulture.

He is kicking me when I am down. He is worse than the police checking up on me.

Emotions

Primary feelings: desperation, helplessness in the face of addiction, depression

Secondary feelings: anger at everyone who wants or reminds you of money

Behavior: lash out and swear at the landlord

Desired behavior:

It is not the landlord's fault. You are kicking him for your mistake. Work out a schedule of payments or deposits so the landlord feels secure, and you do not have big amounts of money to lose in the machines.

Give yourself a score from 1 to 3 on how well you answered on situation # 10:_____

Remember, a score of 1 means you were off on the wrong track; a score of 2 indicates you are doing okay on this situation; a score of 3 means excellent—you should be a counselor!

Respect of Others

Congratulations, you have completed your exercises! You looked, you saw, you struggled with these problems just like every human being. Hopefully, you will not be faced with all or many of these in your actual life. You have gained in some ways. Maybe you did not always come up with the best solutions, but all people have to struggle with some of these problems. However, the important thing is that you have thought about them. You are more prepared, and you have gained one of the great virtues in life . . ."patience."

Instead of immediately flying off the handle as a complete victim to your worst thoughts and emotions, you have become more reflective in your thoughts and more deliberate in your actions. You are becoming one of those people you admire. You are becoming the kind of person who can step back, look at a situation, and figure out what is happening to you and all the others involved. This is the beginning of wisdom. And, with wisdom you gain not only self-respect but also respect from others. Because you know how to react properly with thought and in-sight, you will have the respect of others.

Chapter 7

Revisiting Risk:
An Ounce of Prevention

There is no doubt about it, you are doing a fantastic job! Getting to this part of the book shows your commitment to being a "better you." The rest of this book is a walk through the park! This is true especially now, since you have created your list of Risky Thoughts and Coping Thoughts. That is great! But "great" is not forever. Things change. Situations change. We get into new relationships. We find new friends, and sometimes lose old ones. We move. We get job promotions, demotions, or change jobs completely. We get new neighbors (some good, some bad).

Because change occurs, risks also may change. What used to be risks, with practice and the passage of time, may not be risks any longer. Further, due largely to our changing environment, what were not even considered to be risks for us are now important risks. We need to recognize, identify, and develop some coping thoughts to deal with these new risks properly. Therefore, we suggest that you review or "Revisit your Risk" plan every three months or so. Make the necessary changes. It is a sound and worthwhile investment!

Revisiting Risks Worksheet

(*You may reproduce this sheet.*)

Date: _____

I have taken the time to review my old risky thoughts and have taken into account any new risks, taken time to consider any new coping thoughts, consulted with my "support team," and have come up with the following Current Risk Worksheet.

Current Risk Worksheet

Risky Thoughts   Coping Thoughts

                                        : _____

_____

                                        : _____

_____

Risky Feelings   Coping Feelings
_____

                                        : _____

_____

                                        : _____

_____

Risky Behaviors   Coping Behaviors
_____

                                        : _____

_____

                                        : _____

_____

Risky Places   Coping Places
_____

                                        : _____

_____

                                        : _____

_____

Risky Persons   Coping Persons
_____

                                        : _____

_____

                                        : _____

_____

Be sure to share this new list with your Support Team (described in the next chapter)!

Chapter 8

Your Support Team: Lean on Me

Now, you should feel proud of the progress that you have made concerning your efforts to manage your anger and aggression. You need to take a final risk. You must tell others about your risky thoughts. In fact, give them an actual copy of your risky thoughts and coping thoughts! Just like a quarterback who cannot win a game all by himself, he needs the whole team, on defense as well as on offense, your chances of "winning" may depend on your other "team players."

Of course, do not tell everyone about your plan or list, just those who you care about, those who you feel you can trust, those who you respect, and those who will act in your best interests. These people can watch over you—to protect you from your risks, maybe even protect you from yourself! Give yourself credit. You have made a great deal of progress by coming so far! Think about it. You have identified what thoughts, feelings, behaviors, situations, and so forth place you at risk of becoming angry (and possibly aggressive).

You learned in the first *Cage Your Rage* that only you, yourself, choose to be angry! However, we are not perfect creatures. We tend to be creatures of habit. When the going gets tough, we tend to react by doing what has helped us in the past. If we were aggressive and solved the problem that way, we likely may be tempted to go the easy route and fall back into old habits. After all, it is difficult to practice and use a new skill, especially one that involves our feelings. That is precisely the reason that we need some "risk watchdogs."

These risk watchdogs are the people who care for us, who can tell us when we are starting to slip. Of course, you have to be careful about whom you choose. To help you understand their role, think of the word "SHARE." The first letter of each of the following words sums up what we want these people to do for us. We will see how this word can help you remember the key points about your support team. Other people, who we pick to share our risk list and plan with, can offer us the following, but only if we SHARE with them:

Support us

Honestly advise us

Alert us to problems

Respect us

Encourage us

These people, your friends who are special in your life, can and will offer you support and encouragement as you make your transition into your new lifestyle. You will be selective about whom you share this information with because you have respect for them and they have respect for you. Working together with you, they can alert you to risks that you may not see or realize.

It is very important to pick those people who are special to you. You will supply a copy of your list to these chosen ones. Some suggestions may include:

Mother and/or father

Brother or sister

Spouse

Best friend(s)

Priest or minister

Parole or probation officer

Cousin

Girlfriend/boyfriend

Make sure that you feel comfortable with whomever will be on your list of "risk watchdogs." Be sure that they would likely tell you if they spot trouble. And remember the benefits of SHARE-ing!

Risk Watchdogs

The following individuals are my "risk watchdogs." I will give them a copy of my Risky Thoughts and suggested Coping Thoughts.

1. _____

2. _____

3. _____

4. _____

5. _____

Chapter 9

Released:
Free at Last!

Be Aware!

You have learned many things from this book. You have read and thought about a lot of new material and completed a lot of exercises. The one major point for you to walk away with after reading this book is a simple notion of "being aware." In fact, everything that you have learned in this book is related to the concept of being aware—being aware of your thoughts, feelings, behaviors, certain persons, and situations. It is time for a general review of the things of which you should be aware.

1. Be aware of you anger signs. Know what your thoughts, emotional feelings, physical feelings, and behaviors are when you are becoming angry. By being aware, you will be able to intervene while you still have a fairly cool head about you.

2. Ask yourself, "Why am I feeling this way?"

3. Identify your primary feelings, such as insecurity, confusion, helplessness, hurt, and so forth.

4. Deal with the situation at the primary level. This means being very honest with yourself and with others. Use "I" statements such as, "I am feeling very confused right now, can you please explain this to me?" and follow it up by asking several questions until you can deal better with the situation in a more rational way.

5. If dealing with your feelings at the primary level will not work—for example, if you are too worked up over the situation—try to take a "time-out." Simply explain to the other person that you are too angry to discuss the matter further and that you have to leave for a

period of time to cool down. Arrange for a time that you can meet to further discuss the situation or possible conflict. When you come back, try to deal with things at the primary level.

6. Be aware and use the Relapse Prevention Anger Log! If you use it regularly until you do get a handle on yourself, you will not have to fill it out so often. But go back to using it whenever you realize that things are going wrong for you—that you are becoming angry very often. The key to all of this is to keep being aware of what is occurring.

7. Refer back to your risky business and coping strategies sheet as well as your sabotaging business and coping strategies sheet from time to time to make sure that you are making changes—wherever necessary (as new challenges arise).

Looking over this long list of things mentioned in these chapters, you can get some indication of just how much progress you actually have made. Good for you.

Afterword

Well, you have done it! You managed to make it to the finish line! You made a great deal of effort and showed a lot of motivation making it all the way here. Do not let it all go down the drain!

What did I learn from reading this book and completing the exercises?

_____

_____

_____

_____

_____

_____

_____

_____

_____

One of the ways that you can buy a kind of "insurance policy" for all of the efforts that you have made is by sharing this information with a person who is very close to you—somebody who you trust. Let them see copies of your risky business, sabotaging business, relapse prevention anger logs, anger signs, and so forth. Get some help and support from a close network of people who would be acting in your best interest. It will make the whole process of change easier.

Use the steps outlined in this manual. Using all of the information that you had to write down in this book will help you to remain aware. It also will keep the rage caged!

What additional things can you do to keep your rage caged and to keep from sabotaging your new freedom?

_____

_____

_____

_____

_____

_____

_____

_____

_____